Guitar Music Theory

Fast Track Your Guitar Skills With This Essential Guide to Music Theory & Songwriting For The Guitar. Includes, Songs, Scales, Chords and Much More

Tommy Swindal

© Copyright 2020 - All rights reserved.

The content contained within this book may not be reproduced, duplicated or transmitted without direct written permission from the author or the publisher.

Under no circumstances will any blame or legal responsibility be held against the publisher, or author, for any damages, reparation, or monetary loss due to the information contained within this book, either directly or indirectly.

Legal Notice:

This book is copyright protected. It is only for personal use. You cannot amend, distribute, sell, use, quote or paraphrase any part, or the content within this book, without the consent of the author or publisher.

Disclaimer Notice:

Please note the information contained within this document is for educational and entertainment purposes only. All effort has been executed to present accurate, up to date, reliable, complete information. No warranties of any kind are declared or implied. Readers acknowledge that the author is not engaged in the rendering of legal, financial, medical or professional advice. The content within this book has been derived from various sources. Please consult a licensed professional before attempting any techniques outlined in this book.

By reading this document, the reader agrees that under no circumstances is the author responsible for any losses, direct or indirect, that are incurred as a result of the use of the information contained within this document, including, but not limited to, errors, omissions, or inaccuracies.

Discover "How to Find Your Sound"

http://musicprod.ontrapages.com/

Swindali music coaching/Skype lessons.

Email djswindali@gmail.com for info and pricing

Table of Contents

Introduction
Chapter 1: The Musical Alphabet
  From A to Z
    Musical Notes
    Understanding Key Signatures
Chapter 2: The Guitar
  The Neck
    Mastering the Neck
Chapter 3: Reading Rhythm Charts
  Rhythm 101
    Rhythm Patterns
Chapter 4: Triads, Tones, and Semitones
  The Triads
    Tones and Semitones
Chapter 5: Scales and Keys
  Understanding Scales
    Creating Scales
Chapter 6: The Final Stop
  Chords and Higher
    Songwriting with Modes
Conclusion
References

Introduction

It's natural for a beginner to experience many stops and starts when it comes to learning music theory. I know how intimidating the tables, numbers, and patterns can be, especially if you have never studied music. I never had the chance to study music in highschool or college and had to rely on my dedication to gain this knowledge. Which means I wrote down everything I could find online or in text that I knew would come in handy; this obsessive habit proved helpful. This is why I am confident that what you read here will jump start your creative brain.

My name is Tommy Swindal. I am an experienced composer. I have created music for many years, for many musicians, and as with any story, it has its ups and downs. But I am happy to report that my journey has been successful. I have helped musicians learn to read, understand, and better use music theory to further their career. Although the results were promising, my approach, I felt, was limiting my exposure. It was only after writing books did I realize that this was the best way to reach a wider audience. I may not be able to teach you in person, but I can certainly provide you with everything I know, put down in words.

All of these theories and techniques are applicable regardless of the music you wish to pursue, because they are the very rudimentary basics. Once you understand the concepts of scales, chords, and the other concepts, you can venture on to learn more complex structures and theories on your own with confidence and fluency.

The biggest hurdle any guitarist faces at the start of their career is understanding what they are seeing. Music theory is vast, complex, and truly a language of its own. To fully harness your talents, whether it's a hobby or profession, you must allow yourself to learn the fundamentals. Build upon this base and you will soon be reading music sheets as if written in everyday language.

I find most of the books available today on this topic to be far too bulky and leave the reader no better than where they started. Around 90% of text is long-winded filler, serving no purpose and the remaining 10% is filled with poorly explained concepts, incorrect assumptions, and graphs or charts too difficult to apply to any practice. It's natural as a beginner for music sheets to make your head spin. The solution isn't to avoid, but to learn and face the challenge head on. These concepts are not hard to understand, it just takes time to fully grasp what they mean. If you want to read like a professional and go beyond phone games to play a real guitar, set aside time for yourself and let me teach you.

Here you will be provided with the information you need to get started and take your guitar skills to the next level. I will be focusing only on theories, skills, and techniques essential to learning. You will find clear charts, and tips on how to start writing down tabs and notes in a unique way. This book is ideal for absolute beginners to guitar, as well as those familiar with the basics. I will not leave anything on assumption, meaning if you come across something you think is too complicated to progress, have no fear it will be explained in time.

With that being said, all that remains is to begin our journey through the powerful world of guitar. Let's get riffing!

Chapter 1: The Musical Alphabet

Our journey starts with learning how to read. It is only after having the ability to read can we proceed to write, or in our case, to play the notes and visualize them.

When it comes to learning a language, one must begin with the alphabet. Music, unsurprisingly, is a language that has its own. It is easy to read, memorize, and use later on. In fact, you may already know some of it as it is derived from the English alphabet. The only difference is that instead of 'A' being a character of language, for musicians, 'A' is a note you can play.

Maybe you are someone who knows a few basic chords or strumming patterns while having no idea what notes you are playing, or how you can play a music notation from a sheet with no knowledge of it. The problem is that many of us are in a rush, and we overlook the importance of learning essential theories. By doing so, we arrive at a stage where things start to get too complex, and we are now unable to fully grasp what comes next. Prolong that confusion, and you will likely want to set your guitar aside, thinking it is too much to decipher without help. Sound familiar? Don't worry that is about to change.

From A to Z

Music theory centers around notes, musical notes tuned, and playable on any instrument. From pianos to guitars, clarinet to the violin, all of these musical instruments have notes which they go on to play to create a tune. All of them follow the same universal structure of musical notes.

While it is relatively easy to find notes on a piano because of the differentiating black and white keys, it is a completely different concept when playing the same notes on the guitar. Unlike the piano, where the notes are in a horizontal arrangement, these are all over the place on the guitar's neck.

Musical Notes

A, B, C, D, E, F, G

These are known as natural musical notes. You may be wondering "Did I just read the beginning of the alphabet?" Well yes, but remember they are derived from the English language. This will make things a little easier. Each letter represents a specific note that is played on an instrument with a definitive sound once engaged.

Each note coincides with a flat and a sharp. Sharps are a half-step up whereas the flats are a half-step down and change the note completely. Sharps are denoted by the octothorpe (or number) sign '#' and the flats are denoted by the stylised lowercase 'b' sign. While reading a music sheet, these are made clear. To help with any confusion I have included the seven notes below with their flats and sharps.

A, A#, B, C, C#, D, D#, E, F, F#, G, G#

A few things to notice here:

1. I have never used flats in the above sequence of notes. Why? Because that is only used when you are half-

stepping down, or in the case of a guitar, backward. Since we are only going forward, I used the above.
2. There isn't any 'sharp' for B and E. That is a special case; keep this in mind.

Now, let us write this backward, starting from G#, all the way to A.

Ab, G, Gb, F, E, Eb, D, Db, C, B, Bb, A

The notes B, and E, both have natural sounds that if you use a half-step, they would immediately change to the next one. Similarly, if you wish to switch to a half-step down, the other notes will no longer have flats. Now that we have that sorted, it is time to learn how to read notations.

Understanding Key Signatures

To begin with, let's look at a music sheet sample with a typical arrangement. From there, we will learn what some of these symbols mean, and how to read the notes. Do not worry about playing them yet, I will take you through that in the next chapter.

First things first. The staff is where music is written. The staff consists of five lines with four spaces in between.

See the symbol? That is a treble clef. What makes this unique is the position of the circle that overlaps the vertical line. For guitars, this is supposed to be at this position, because it is at this position that the note 'G' is played.

How do you know what note to play? Start with the bottom line, or 'E.' Moving up to the first space, that is the note 'F.' Then 'G' comes in on the second line. This is the same line where a circle is placed within the symbol. Next space is 'A', and you get the idea. Of course, it can be hard to remember where to begin and where to end. To make things a little easier to remember, use this trick:

- **For spaces** - In the correct order, the word 'FACE' should appear. Always remember that the gaps are reserved for F, A, C, E.
- **For lines** - The sentence "**E**very **G**ood **B**oy **D**oes **F**ine" is a perfect way to remember that the notes, highlighted in bold characters, are what appear on the line.

Now, you might be wondering where the sharp and flat symbols are? When a piece requires the note to sound sharp, you will see the '#' sign before the letter This means, if your piece includes a C# note, the symbol on the position of C will have a sharp sign before it.

For flats, it is the same. The symbol, which is identical to the lowercase letter 'b' will be displayed before the note. This would indicate that you would need to step half-down from your current note to execute the sound properly.

Finally, both of these signs are in effect, until a natural note sign is used. This would return the notes to normal. Here is an image to show these three symbols in action.

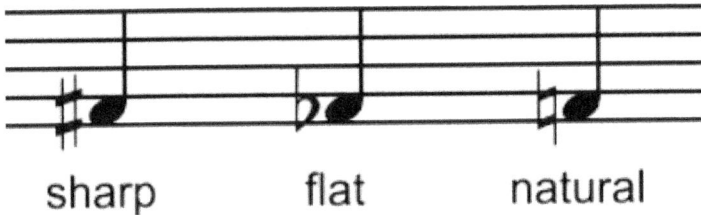

sharp   flat   natural

You will not be seeing the natural tone much, but it is important to know going forward and reading music.

The staff is divided into sections called measures. You will be able to spot these easily as they are the only vertical lines or bar lines.

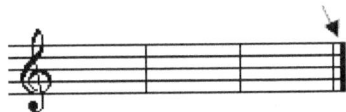

Notice that at the end of the staff, there is a thicker bar line. This is a double bar line, and it is meant to indicate the end of a piece.

There will be times where you may come across two dots at the start and the end of a measure or a piece. These dots indicate this section is meant to repeat. Everything in the middle of these dots will be played again, and this is common in songs and melodies.

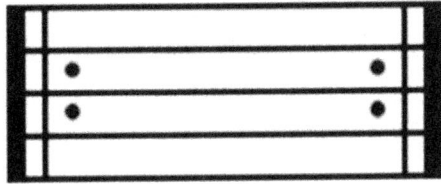

While most professional musicians have sheets representing the music in a standard staff, there is one more version you may encounter. You can work with either of these, or if you wish to mix things up, use both at the same time.

The image below shows a typical sheet using the standard staff method, and another version called tablature. It is meant to be used when notes are fingered, and commonly used for stringed instruments.

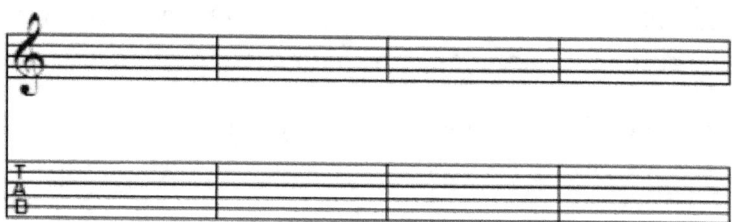

A few things you should note here:

1. Just as we use the treble clef for staff notations, we use the word 'TAB' for tablature.
2. The staff has five lines, and it uses the spaces. The tab version only uses the lines, and each line represents a single string on a guitar.
3. Unlike the staff, where notes are represented using symbols, the tablature uses numbers to indicate the fret position of a specific string on the neck. This takes away the guesswork.

I will show you more about how to use tabs in the next chapter. In the meantime, let's familiarize ourselves with symbols, what they mean, and how to play them.

Symbols

Each symbol on the staff, after the initial treble clef, provides information about the note that is to be played. Each of these symbols holds different meanings, providing more details about how you must play the note. It is ideal for getting familiar with these symbols as they will help you develop more understanding about music composition and you will perform better.

All of these symbols represent individual notes. Every note that is played comes with a head, stem, and flag.

Head

If you come across a note head, which is oval in shape, it will be either black or white. In music theory, they are referred to as filled or open, respectively. These heads sit on their respective positions on the staff, providing information about the note. So when you come across the note, look for the position of the head. If the head is on 'A' the corresponding note must be played.

Stem

The stem is a thin line that stretches from the note head vertically upwards or downwards, depending on the note's position. Do not be confused by these two as they do not affect the way you play these notes. These just provide you with references.

The lines that go upwards start from the right side of the head, and the ones that go down begin from the left. Once again, this does not affect anything. Any note that falls at or above the 'B' line will have a downward-facing stem.

Flag

The flag is just like it sounds. It is a curved line that extends from the tip of the stem to the right. The purpose of the flag, however, is very important. The flags indicate how long the note must be held. A single flag shortens the duration while multiple flags shorten these further.

Values

Note values are essentially the duration of the note itself. Let us refer back to the filled and open notes to understand this better. The key below shows some of these values.

```
♩ ♩ ♩ ♩  =  ♩ ♩  =  o
1 2 3 4     1 2 3 4     1 2 3 4
4 Quarter Notes   2 Half Notes   1 Whole Note
```

In the image above, we have four quarter notes. These are represented using filled notes with stems. If you were to tap your foot four times in a loop, every tap would require you to a single quarter note.

Next, we have the half notes. These are represented with open heads with stems. One half note takes two beats, meaning that you can play this note twice on a beat of four.

Finally, we have the whole note. This, as the name suggests, must be played and held throughout the loop of the beat. You do not need to play it again unless required afterward.

Dots

You might often come across notes which have dots placed next to them. These can be a bit tricky to understand at first, but easy to execute if you practice. The dot that follows the note head adds half of that specific note's duration to the playtime. So, if you come across a half note with a dot, you would play that note for three beats instead of two.

Tie

There will be times when you need to hold a note you played as the last note of the previous measure. When switching to the new measure, the same note must be held in place. To represent this, a tie is used. This is simply a curved line above the notes, and generally between the measure bars, to show that the two notes are tied together.

The chart below shows how a tie looks like:

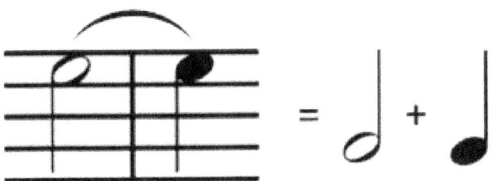

Tied notes: Holding the first note until the duration of both is complete

While the above are mostly methods to prolong the notes or extend duration, the opposite is also possible. Flags or beams are generally used to signify shortened durations of the notes that are to be played. To give you an idea of what you can expect to see in music sheets to know when you need to play notes shorter, or faster, look at the image below:

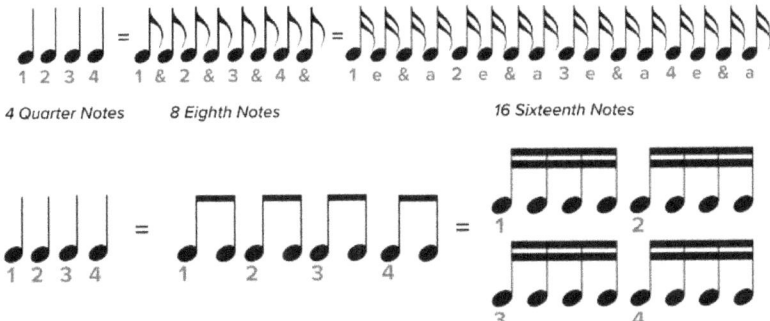

In both the examples above, notes have been shortened from their regular durations. In the first instance, the quarter notes have been shortened in duration to play twice as much within the same time limit. You would normally play a single quarter note per beat, but now you would play it twice per beat if the flag shows one curved line. If it shows two, you will need to shorten the duration further so you can play four notes within a single beat, which is easier said than done.

Similarly, in the next image, you see beams being used. These function the same way as the flags. The above illustration shows exactly the same pace as before. Just remember:

Single beams or single flags halve the time value of a note. Double beams or double flags make it one-fourth of the time value of a note.

Rests

There will be times where you may not have any notes to play, or that you deliberately introduce some rest. These occurrences are denoted with appropriate rest symbols. Shown below are the types of rests you can encounter during your musical performance.

Time Signature

Every staff comes with a time signature. This is to set the beat of the song or piece in question. Immediately after the treble clef symbol, you will come across two numbers. Generally, these are four and four, but in some cases, they can vary.

The number above shows how many beats you need to complete a measure. The number below shows the performer the exact note value for every beat. This is the pulse of your foot tapping along the rhythm as you listen.

Remember the metronome I mentioned? This is where it comes in. To give you every idea of how these beats are to be managed, how you need to play your notes, and when, you use a metronome to guide you throughout pieces you intend to play.

Key Signatures

Finally, it is time to learn the all-important key signatures. Without these, you may end up playing the entire piece wrong.

The key signatures are extremely important details that are to be taken into account before you start playing. A key signature is vital information placed right after the treble clef, which can either be a sharp or a flat. This denotes that the entire piece, you will need to use either sharp or flat for specific notes. Here is a list of flats and sharp key signatures you will often find to give you a better idea:

Sharps

G major - One sharp symbol

D major - Two sharp symbols

A major - Three sharp symbols

E major - Four

B major - Five

F# major - Six

C# major - Seven

Flats

F major - One flat symbol

Bb major - Two flat symbols

Eb major - Three flat symbols

Ab major - Four

Db major - Five

Gb major - Six

Cb major - Seven

Easy to forget, so I would suggest you write these down. Before I go on, here are some other names worth mentioning as you might come across, and they can be difficult to remember.

- Semibreve - whole note
- Minim - half note
- Crotchet - quarter note
- Quaver - eighth note
- Semiquaver - sixteenth note
- Time - beat information

That wasn't so bad, was it? A pat on the back for you for making it this far. In the next chapter, we will be diving right into guitar. Flex your muscles, stretch a little if you like, because we are about to start playing some music.

Chapter 2: The Guitar

Ah, how I love my guitars. I still remember when I bought my first one, I had no idea what to look for. Luckily, I had help from someone who knew about guitars, allowing me to save money and buy a good one worthy of my time.

Even though the instrument looks sleek, sounds beautiful and crisp, there are still quite a few things you need to know to make full use of the guitar, and play it the way it is meant to be.

Just strumming a chord or two is not enough, nor is shredding a mindless solo piece worth the effort. If you do not understand the delicacies involved, you will never learn to appreciate music's real nature. This is why many musicians fail, despite having incredible skill. They do not bother to learn theory or technique, which enhances the experiences for the performer and listener. They may know what note to play by sound, but they don't know which note they are playing, why a specific chord is shaped the way it is, or what an octave is, and that can be a problem.

In this chapter, we aren't looking to learn the anatomy of a guitar, we will focus our attention on the most vital part: the neck. It is on the neck where we find each note, right and wrong. It is the neck that contains the fretboard.

The Neck

I am sure you know what frets are at this point, but just in case you are starting from the beginning, let us refresh our memory a bit.

The standard guitar, acoustic or otherwise, has six strings. All of these strings run from the top, through the neck and the fretboard, and right into the bridge, where they are held together. These strings have a name assigned to them, and that is something every guitarist must know.

Starting from the fattest string often referred to as the sixth string, we have the 'E' string. Moving forward, we have 'A,' 'D,' 'G,' 'B,' and 'e.' Notice the last one is denoted with a small 'e' and that is to signify that you are using the thinnest string on the guitar.

You will soon be able to remember them easily if you tune your guitar using tuners. These names are essentially the notes they play when they are plucked without pressing a fret position. Playing a string with any fretted note plays an open note. This means each string should play their respective notes on an open position. If any of these sounds slightly off, use a tuner. Now comes the interesting part. If you recall, I mentioned you could use the tablature form to play your tunes. As a practice, here is your first look at how a typical tablature would work.

In the table below, you will find both the tab form and the standard staff arrangement. Try and play the sequence below.

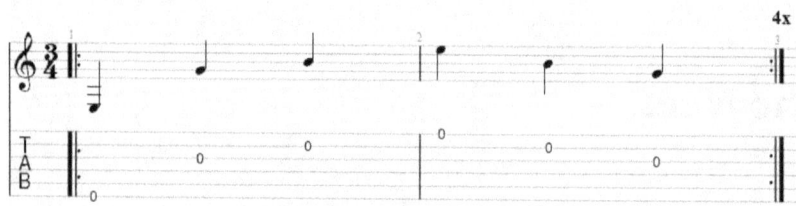

Whether you play it using the staff or the tabs, the result is exactly the same. Notice that this piece uses a repeat, and the number of times you need to play these two measures is indicated as '4x' which means you will need to play these measures four times.

Go ahead, give it a go.

Recognize the song you are playing? That is the intro for Metallica's song *Nothing Else Matters.* Coming from a band that is known for some of the craziest rhythms and solos, this one is rather simple.

All of the notes shown above are on open strings. The lowest line on the tab is your 'E' string, the thickest one. Similarly, to indicate the exact octave and position of this note, additional lines are drawn in the staff to match the note.

The notes you just played above are:

E, G, B, e, B, G - Four times

It helps if you memorize the chart below that shows all the notes and their corresponding positions on the fretboard. It would also allow you to clarify some other concepts, such as octave, scales, chords, etc.

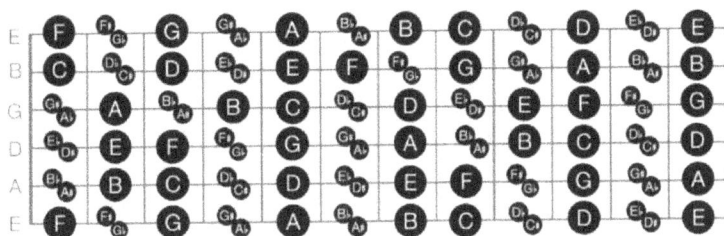

The above starts from the left and stretches to the right. These are 12 fret positions for each string on a guitar. Although the guitar has more than 12 frets, we will be limiting ourselves to just 12 for now, making it simple.

After every 12 notes, the octave ends, and the notes start all over again. Take the 'A' string, as shown above, as a good way to learn. The zero position or the open position of this string will play the note 'A.' With every fret you press, the note changes. This continues until you arrive at the 12th fret, where you find 'A' once again. The only difference here would be the octave.

Memorizing the fretboard will also help figure out where your notes are when performing, or writing songs. You can play solos, make chords, find entry and exit points for leads, and so much more.

Mastering the Neck

A good way to get a good command on the neck and visualize where these notes are, let's do a note finding exercise.

I will provide you with three tasks or notes. Your job is to find these notes on the map and play them with a metronome. You can set the tempo to as low as 40 beats per minute (bpm). The idea is to familiarize yourself with all the positions of the same note before the 12th fret.

Task 1: Starting from the sixth E string (the thickest one), find and play all the 'F' notes on all strings, one by one. Make sure you do not cross the 12th fret.

Task 2: Similar to the above, find and play all the C# notes.

Task 3: Find and play all the G notes.

A quick tip: For beginners, an easy way to identify the 12th fret is to look at the edge of your guitar's neck. Where you spot two dots, that fret is your 12th fret.

From here, you can start mixing some notes or choose your own to practice on. You would know that you are comfortable once you can play the notes without looking at the guitar. Once that happens, add in a note to make it a pair. For example, finding both G and A, and playing them one after the other.

These tips and exercises are great to familiarize yourself with notes on the neck and to figure out if you are playing the correct note by visualizing the sound and position without actually looking.

This brings us to the end of this chapter. It may have been shorter, but we have done the hard part. What follows may also seem hard, but with enough practice it will be a piece of cake, and soon you'll be writing your own songs like a professional.

Chapter 3: Reading Rhythm Charts

Rhythm is elegant, harmonious, and necessary. Without rhythm, a song isn't a song. Even the most powerful lyrics and complimentary music would not feel right if there was no rhythm to make it flow.

Since we are more interested in learning about guitar rhythms, they serve this purpose. You can play a song without a drum, metronome, or even a beat, as long as you can maintain a rhythmic chord progression. This is the beauty that can only be seen in guitars. Unlike any other instrument, the guitar alone can create incredible chord progressions and provide rhythms at the same time. It also allows singers and performers to match the tempo and sing accordingly.

Reading rhythms does not necessarily mean you will be studying chords, but you may, at times, be required to continue or maintain a rhythm while playing a solo. In either case, a guitarist needs to know how to read rhythm. Fortunately, it is a lot easier than it sounds.

Rhythm 101

On the staff, we need two essential pieces of information.

1. Pitch
2. Rhythm

Luckily, we know both of them. The first one can be found by locating the head of the note on the staff. This would provide us with the note, or pitch, that needs to be played.

The rhythm comes in the form of the time value of these notes. The stems and flags are where we get rhythm. If your piece has a time of 4/4, and you are presented with four quarter notes, you will play it accordingly. If you are given eighth notes instead, you will need to speed up your playing to match the rhythm.

A good way to start working on rhythm is to first understand the time signature for the piece you are about to play. If your piece has 4/4, count the beat, tap your foot, or use a metronome to help you out. I personally find that counting helps a lot of beginners.

"1, 2, 3, 4" can be used when you are playing whole notes, half notes, or even the quarter notes. The lower value in a time signature shows how many quarter notes can be played in a measure. Since our example piece uses the value of four, we will only use four quarter notes.

"1, and 2, and 3, and 4" tends to work best when playing eighth notes. These are half as short as quarter note durations. This means you will have a rhythm where you play two notes in a single beat. The result would see you play a total of eight, but more on that later. Just remember, you do not need to play all the eight notes in a measure as it all depends on the rhythm you are trying to achieve.

"1, e, &, a, 2, e, &, a, 3, e &, a, 4, e &, a" is a popular way many guitarists use to count the notes or beats within a measure when playing the sixteenth notes. By the end of this sentence, you would have played 16 notes, at most.

The idea behind these silly ways of "say as you play" is to count. The sooner you get into this habit, the easier it would be for you to play complex rhythms.

Just a few lines ago, I mentioned that the rhythm does not mean that you will play all the notes in a measure, to meet the time signature. There may be places where you need to sustain notes or take a rest. This deliberate pause/stop and play is what creates a more lively rhythm.

We spoke a little about rests earlier as well. However, when it comes to rhythm, it is essential to identify the type of rest symbol you are looking at when performing or composing music pieces.

Just like the type of notes, you also have various types of rests. Below is an illustration of these rests and their respective types.

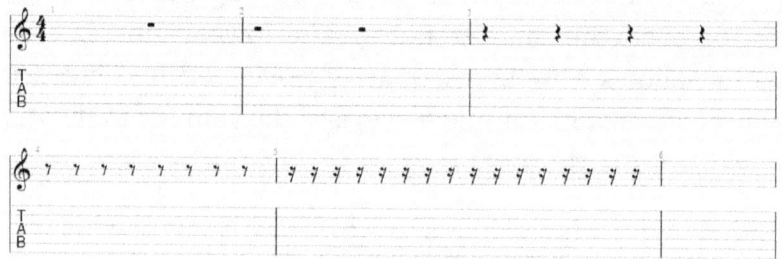

Rests used for rhythms

Starting from the first measure, we have the whole note rest. A dash indicates this under a corresponding line. The rest duration for this would be the whole measure, or all four beats.

Next, we have the half-note rest. This sits right on top of its corresponding line. Unlike the above, this rests above, not below its line.

Tip: To remember which rest means what, think of, "A whole gentleman takes his hat off (downwards), while the half-gentleman keeps his hat on (upwards).

Moving forward, we have the quarter rests. Each rest symbol means resting for a quarter of the measure, or one beat only.

Following the quarter rest is the eighth note rest. Finally, we have the sixteenth note rest, and both of these serve the same duration as the notes.

Here is another exercise for you. Try and play the piece shown in the image below. You can then go on to change the notes and rests to your preferred time values. Remember that you will need to use the corresponding rest symbols, to ensure that you do not end up breaking the rhythm.

In the above exercise, you will see that I have used chords. While it is one thing to read chords in tablature form, it is slightly tricky to read these in staff notations. Luckily, you will be able to see the names of these chords either above or below their first occurrences and sometimes in each one.

Practice playing the above, and use any tempo of your choice. Start slowly, and then start picking up pace. You can later change these from quarter notes and rests to whole notes, half notes, and eighths, or if you fancy a bit of a challenge, go for the sixteenth notes.

Rhythm Patterns

When performing a rhythm, you will often come across symbols which further indicate what type of stroke you need to use, or any special technique that you may need that applies to rhythms. Generally, there are three which are used widely. The chart below shows these three types, along with their designated symbols.

⊓ = **Downstroke**

V = **Upstroke**

✗ = **Mute**

If you come across these in a music sheet, you can easily carry out the desired action. While the first two are simple, the third one takes a bit of practice. Use your palm to mute notes or chords while strumming to give your rhythm a more enhanced feel.

Varying between downstrokes and upstrokes is referred to as alternate picking, and this technique will come in great use, especially when you are pulling off solos, or trying to play scales. You can also use alternate picking for rhythmic effects. In the exercise above, try and apply varying strokes and alternate picking to see how that changes the sound of your rhythm.

The muted strum is generally a strum of chords or picking notes that are deliberately muted to create a percussive sound that further complements the rhythm. You can try this technique in place of the rest stops we saw earlier.

We have the rhythms sorted, neck memorized, and most of the music sheet jargon out of the way. Now it's time to kick things up a notch and get into the technical aspects of music theory.

Chapter 4: Triads, Tones, and Semitones

Right away, I am not referring to the notoriously infamous triads you see in movies. We are focusing on the type of triads used in the world of music theory.

These are important, worth knowing, and can certainly add in multiple layers of flavor, feel, and experience to the song you are writing. The triad is relatively easy to understand, learn, and practice, and the results are compelling. We will look into various forms of triads, and we will also discover the power of arpeggios within this chapter.

The Triads

A chord is a combination of three or more notes that are played simultaneously. Certain chords use only three notes, arranged as thirds called triads.

Since there are three notes, set as thirds, each of them bears an identification. The note at the bottom is called root, the one in the middle is the third, and the top is the fifth. Triads come in many forms. Some good ones to know are:

- Major
- Minor
- Augmented

- Diminished
- Inversion

Learning these five alone would greatly improve your guitar skills, and the overall music you will play. Let us look into each one of these to better understand how they work.

Major

The major triad is where the chord is created using a root note (1), combining it with a major third (3), and a perfect fifth (5) of a major scale. To give you a better idea, have a look at the example below:

G A B C D E

Using the notes above, we can start constructing a major triad. The root would be 'G' followed by the third and the perfect fifth. This means the complete major triad would be:

G B D

You can use the same rule to create other major triads of your own.

Minor

The rule is pretty much the same here, except for two changes.

1. We use a minor scale.
2. The middle note, the thirds, is flat or half step down (b3).

To create a minor triad, follow the same pattern:

A B C D E F

Since we need to take the root (1), the minor third (b3) and the perfect fifth (5), the result should be:

A C E

That would be your minor triad. You can use the same rule to create other minor triads as you please.

Diminished

The diminished triad is slightly different from the ones we saw above. The diminished triad consists of the root, a minor third (b3), and a diminished fifth (b5). In simpler terms, it is a minor triad with a lower fifth note.

Now, using the above rule, let us create a diminished triad using the notes below:

B C D E F G A

Try and see if you can create this one. I am sure you would be able to figure this out easily now.

The answer is:

B D F

Augmented

The augmented triad uses root note (1), a major third (3), and an augmented fifth (#5). You may have noticed the sharp sign, and you would be correct to assume that this note is played with a sharp tone. The fifth note must be played half a step above, or one fret higher.

C D E F G A

Using these notes, if we were to create an augmented triad, we would end up with:

C E G#

Using the same rule, you can use any root note throughout the neck and create an augmented triad.

Inversion

This is where things get a little tricky. Generally, the root note serves as the bass note as well. However, some chords allow us to change the root note's position from the bottom to the middle or even the top note. Such triads are called inversion triads.

Let us look at an example of the C major triad. The root is C, of course, followed by E and then G. Here, the bass is the root note.

If you switch the place of the bass note to the top, the bass note now becomes the third note, which is E. This inverted chord is then named C/E. You can carry on with another inversion, and to do that, you will replace the E to the top now, which was acting as the bass note, leaving G as your new bass note. Now, the chord becomes C/G.

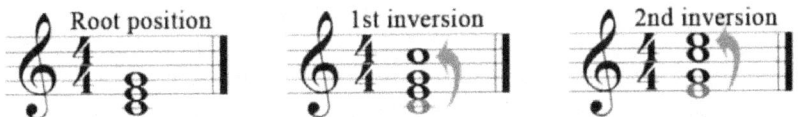

The beauty of triads is that you can construct all kinds of triads using any note as the root throughout the guitar's neck. To get into practice, try and make at least five different triads. Use variations of major, minor, diminished, and inversion, wherever you can. This would further strengthen the concepts and allow you to find better ways to play the guitar, compose songs, and get better as you go along.

You can incorporate your rhythms with triads. Choose a selection of triads of your choice, and redo the exercise we went through in the last chapter. However, instead of using the Em and the D chords, use triads instead. Who knows, you may just come across something new and exciting.

Apart from rhythms, you can also use triads for leads. Depending on the scale of your song, you can use the root, the thirds, and the fifths accordingly to quickly navigate and produce some pleasing and moving leads. Let your creativity flow, and let your music speak to you.

Triad Arpeggios

Surely, there will be times where you may need to improvise, adjust, or modify the piece slightly to make it sound even better. It could be a song you are practicing, and you may feel like it could use something a little better. That is where arpeggios come in.

Arpeggios are your best friends if you wish to carry out improvisation. Every great jazz player loves and uses these every single time. Arpeggios are extensively used, and the reason behind that is that arpeggios only use notes from the chord being played. When that happens, you create a more harmonized sound, making the entire piece different.

Triad arpeggios can be used with all forms of triads we came across earlier. Below you will find triad arpeggio shapes for major, augmented, and diminished triads. The thing to note here is that the root note is shown as 'R' while the third note is '3' and the fifth as '5'.

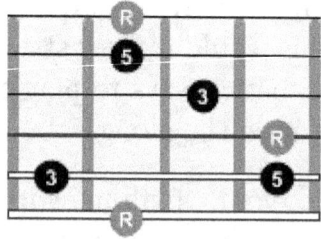

Major Triad Arpeggio

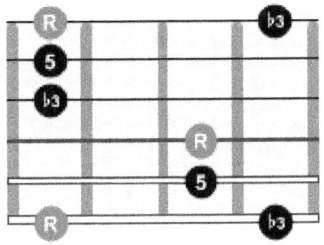

Minor Triad Arpeggio

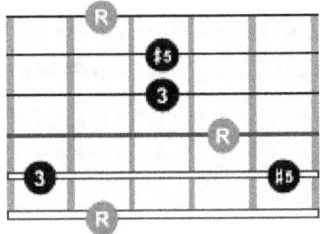

Augmented Triad Arpeggio

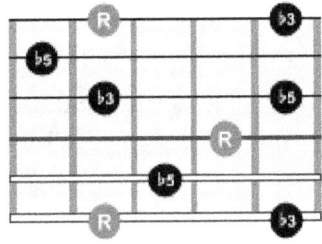

Diminished Triad Arpeggio

Since we are talking about arpeggios and improvisation, you do not need to play these in a specific order. Normally, beginners play the sequence as they create it, as shown below:

1 - 3 - 5

When it comes to using arpeggios, you can alter the sequence, as per your needs. The outcome can be:

1 - 5- 3

3 - 1 - 5

3 - 5 - 1

5 - 1 - 3

5 - 3 - 1

In any of these cases, you are still playing the same triad, but in a different sequence. That is the beauty of arpeggios. You can play notes using any sequence you like, as long as it does not alter the scale or shift into a different triad.

Tones and Semitones

When you play a note on a guitar, and then move up a single fret, or half-note, it is called a semitone. When you move up two frets or a full step, it is called tone. I bring this up because you may come across certain pieces that use tones and semitones as opposed to half-step or whole-step. The latter are generally used within the US.

It is also good to know that as you execute a whole-step, you are skipping a fret. That, in music theory, is referred to as an interval. Simply put, an interval equals two semitones, which results in a tone.

There will be times when you may practice songs or pieces composed elsewhere. It is good to know the difference so you do not get lost during a performance. With that said, it is time to learn about the all-important scales. You need them, you want them, and above all, you cannot make great music without them.

Chapter 5: Scales and Keys

Scales are essentially a sequence of various notes ordered by pitch. That is the easiest explanation I can come up with. However, as you dive deeper into the world of scales, you will discover immense possibilities and complexities, all of which will push you forward to become a better musician and guitarist.

Understanding Scales

The best part now is we no longer need to learn complex theories. All that remains is to glide through some terminology, and play to understand how they work. You already know about symbols, notes, rests, and even rhythm. The rest should be about practice, and nothing more.

Key

A key is the root note of a scale, as it sounds. In the previous chapter about triads, the key serves the same purpose. It acts as the root for the entire scale that is being played.

If you play C, D, and G on your guitar, you are essentially playing the C scale, and you can say that these notes have been derived from the key of C.

Keys play an important role when it comes to scales. It is through these keys that scales are derived. A key can be one of the seven pitches or notes we learned about at the beginning.

The scale notes are "taken directly out of that key" (Guitar Chalk Magazine, 2017).

The scales go on to use the root note, also known as 'tonic,' of the scale sequence. Once you have identified the scale and the key, you can then move a segment or the scale to any position on the fretboard. This would effectively change the key as well.

Major and Minor Scales

Remember "Do, re, mi, fa, so, la, ti, do" you would sometimes sing in school? That is a major scale. That is how you learn to hear a major scale, and it couldn't be more useful here.

Major scales and minor scales are easy to remember. If you learn the basic rule and the five natural positions of both major and minor scales, you should be able to play these with ease, as long as you know what root key you are targeting.

A major scale contains seven notes, and it starts with the root note (1). It goes on in the order given below:

1 2 3 4 5 6 7 + 8

The eighth note is the octave, meaning you will be playing the root note on every eighth note. Minor scales, on the other hand, follow a slightly different pattern. They start the same way, with the root note, but then things change as shown under:

1 2 b3 4 5 b6 b7

This means the scale would have a minor third, minor sixth, and a minor seventh note. Once again, nothing that sounds too complicated. Let us now look at the five natural positions for major scales first, and see how the rule above takes shape.

For illustration, we will be using G major scales. You can change the root note, or move around the fretboard freely, as long as you maintain the same pattern. It is also referred to as the CAGED shape. It is derived from C, A, G, E, and D chord shapes, which can then be moved to play at all the 12 fret positions of the neck. This is done by taking the open chord shapes and closing them, ensuring that no open string is used in the chord. It takes practice, but once you get the hang of these shapes, you should switch between positions freely.

E Shape

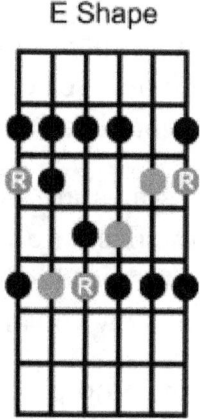

G major scale in E Shape (Klaus Crow, 2014a)

D Shape

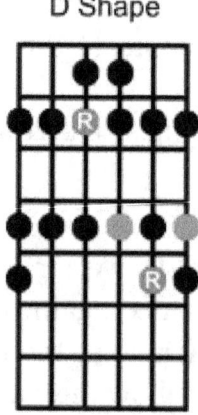

G major in D shape

C Shape

G major in C shape

A Shape

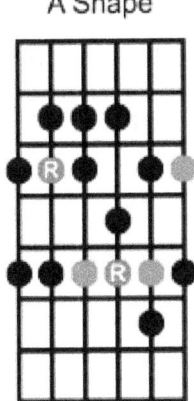

G major in A shape

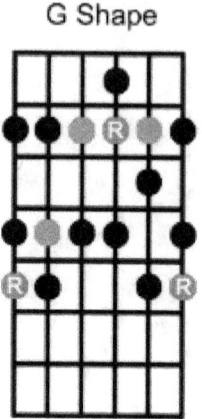

G major in G Shape

Here is a bit of a challenge. Try and change the root key to C, and play at least three positions using the new key.

Remember not to rush through these positions. It is time-consuming and will test your patience. Play these slowly until you have fully memorized these patterns and can play these fluently.

Now comes the interesting bit, shaping the minor scales. The minor scales do not follow the CAGED shapes, which is why they are a bit different. Once again, we will be using five natural minor shapes. If you wish to have a bit of a challenge, try and figure out the position on your own using the rule mentioned above. Do not worry if you get it wrong, as I will be sharing these now.

For the illustration below we will be using A minor as our key.

Position 1

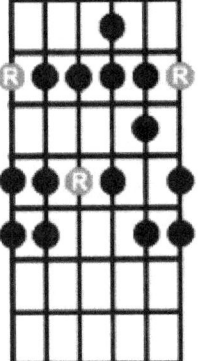

Position 2

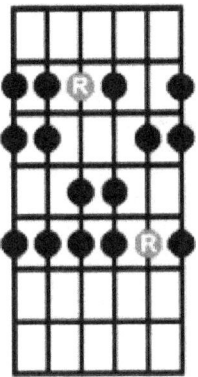

Position 3

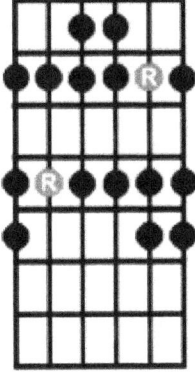

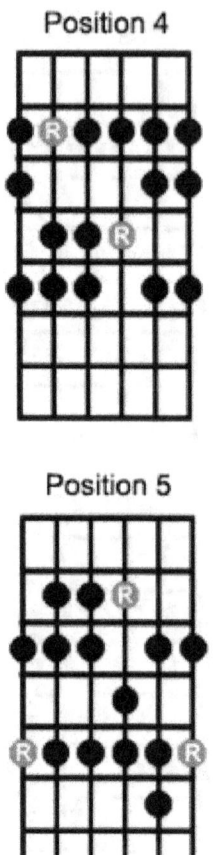

The five positions of A minor scales (Klaus Crow, 2014b)

Using these, you can move around on the scales, whether pursuing a major or a minor scale. Your skills will significantly improve if you can execute these to perfection. The patterns remain the same; all that changes is the key.

Pentatonic Scales

These are perhaps one of the most commonly used and easiest to remember. You can use these for any note, at any position of the neck with ease.

As the name suggests, it contains five notes. There are major pentatonic scales and minor pentatonic scales. Both of them include the same note intervals, which means the pattern remains the same for both. All you need is to learn a new root note.

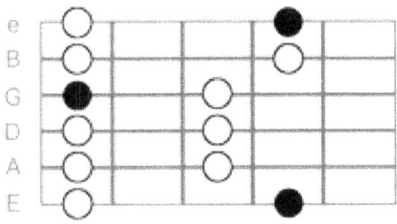

G Major Pentatonic Box Pattern

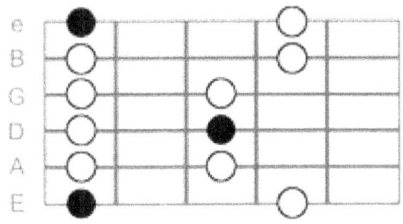

E minor pentatonic box pattern

The black notes represent the root notes. The pattern remains the same. The above is what you call a box pattern, and it derives its root from the CAGED chords. There are other variants of pentatonic in existence, such as:

- Single octave box patterns
- Diagonal major pentatonic scale
- Diagonal minor pentatonic scale

You can always learn these after you have mastered the basic pentatonic scales. They help in playing, and they can be incredibly fun to execute.

Creating Scales

If you wish to create major scales on specific strings, you can use the formula given below, and you will soon be playing your favorite major scale on any chord without hesitation.

W-W-H-W-W-W-H

In the above rule, the 'W' stands for a whole-step (two frets) or one interval. So if you wish to create a G major scale on the E string (sixth string), the notes should be:

G A B C D E F# G (1, 2, 3, 4, 5, 6, 7, 8 or 1)

To construct minor scales on any string, you will need to follow the rule shown below:

W-H-W-W-H-W-W

Try and play a C minor scale on a string of your choice. You can follow the same rule on any string you choose, as long as you start with the root note or the key of the scale.

Intervals

When it comes to scales, intervals do play a role that every musician must understand. While we know intervals are the spaces between the frets, there are instances where intervals are formed by using different combinations.

Before we look at the major and minor scale intervals, it is important to familiarize ourselves with the basics, and that is where the chromatic scale intervals come in. The chart below shows the intervals on a guitar fretboard for a chromatic scale. We will be using 'F' as the root note.

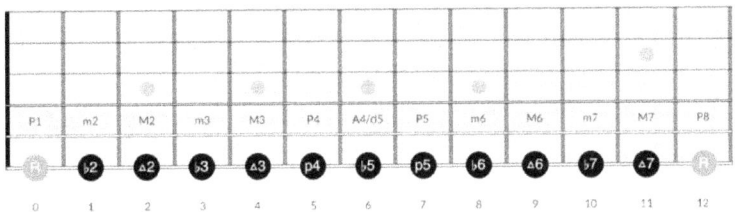

The P1 stands for unison, the lowercase 'm' for minor, and uppercase 'M' for major. The perfect fourth is represented by the P4, augmented fourth or diminished fifth by A4/d5. P8 represents the octave.

Major scales only use major intervals, and those are the second, third, sixth, and seventh, and perfect intervals, which are unison, fourth, fifth, and the octave. The interval names correspond to the scale degree number. Slightly confusing? I know. Let us look at the table below to get a better understanding of how these intervals work.

Note Names:	C to C	C to D	C to E	C to F	C to G	C to A	C to B	C to C
Scale Degree Names:	Tonic	Tonic to Supertonic	Tonic to Mediant	Tonic to Subdominant	Tonic to Dominant	Tonic to Submediant	Tonic to Leading Tone	Tonic to Tonic
Scale Degree Numbers:	1 to 1	1 to 2	1 to 3	1 to 4	1 to 5	1 to 6	1 to 7	1 to 1 (8)
Interval Name:	Unison	Major 2nd	Major 3rd	Perfect 4th	Perfect 5th	Major 6th	Major 7th	Octave
Abbreviation:	-	M2	M3	P4	P5	M6	M7	Oct, 8ve
Half Steps:	0	2	4	5	7	9	11	12

For minor scales, the chart varies just a little.

Note Names:	A to A	A to B	A to C	A to D	A to E	A to F	A to G	A to high A
Scale Degree Names:	Tonic	Tonic to Supertonic	Tonic to Mediant	Tonic to Subdominant	Tonic to Dominant	Tonic to Submediant	Tonic to Subtonic	Tonic to Tonic
Scale Degree Numbers:	1 to 1	1 to 2	1 to 3	1 to 4	1 to 5	1 to 6	1 to 7	1 to 1 (8)
Interval Name:	Unison	Major 2nd	Minor 3rd	Perfect 4th	Perfect 5th	Minor 6th	Minor 7th	Octave
Abbreviation:	-	M2	m3	P4	P5	m6	m7	Oct, 8ve
Half Steps:	0	2	3	5	7	8	10	12

There are multiple scale variations in existence, and we will be looking at some in the next chapter as well as:

- Chord charts
- Useful chord shapes
- Pentatonic scales
- Harmony
- Circle of fourth/fifth

Keep practicing and remember, these rules allow you to explore your potential and creativity fully. The more you practice, the better you get over time.

Chapter 6: The Final Stop

You have made it so far! It fills me with confidence about your practice knowing you can keep up the pace and follow along. This also means that now I can dive into some higher-level components, all of which are designed to make your playing better. Without further ado, let's dive straight into the practical aspects of guitar music theory.

Chords and Higher

We already know what chords are, but just knowing them is not enough. You should also be able to read the chord charts. These are easy to read as they provide almost all the information you need, in terms of position and fret numbers. You need to know a little about how to read these and know which finger presses which fret. Getting the position right is important as doing it any other way would make it very hard to play chords and often give you an aching arm and wrist.

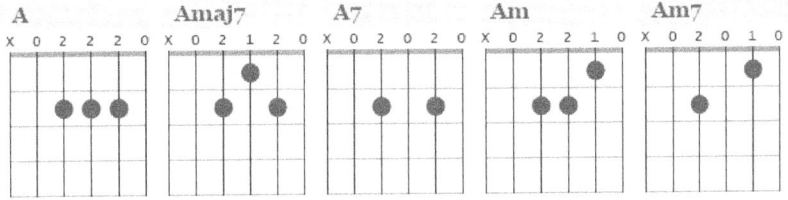

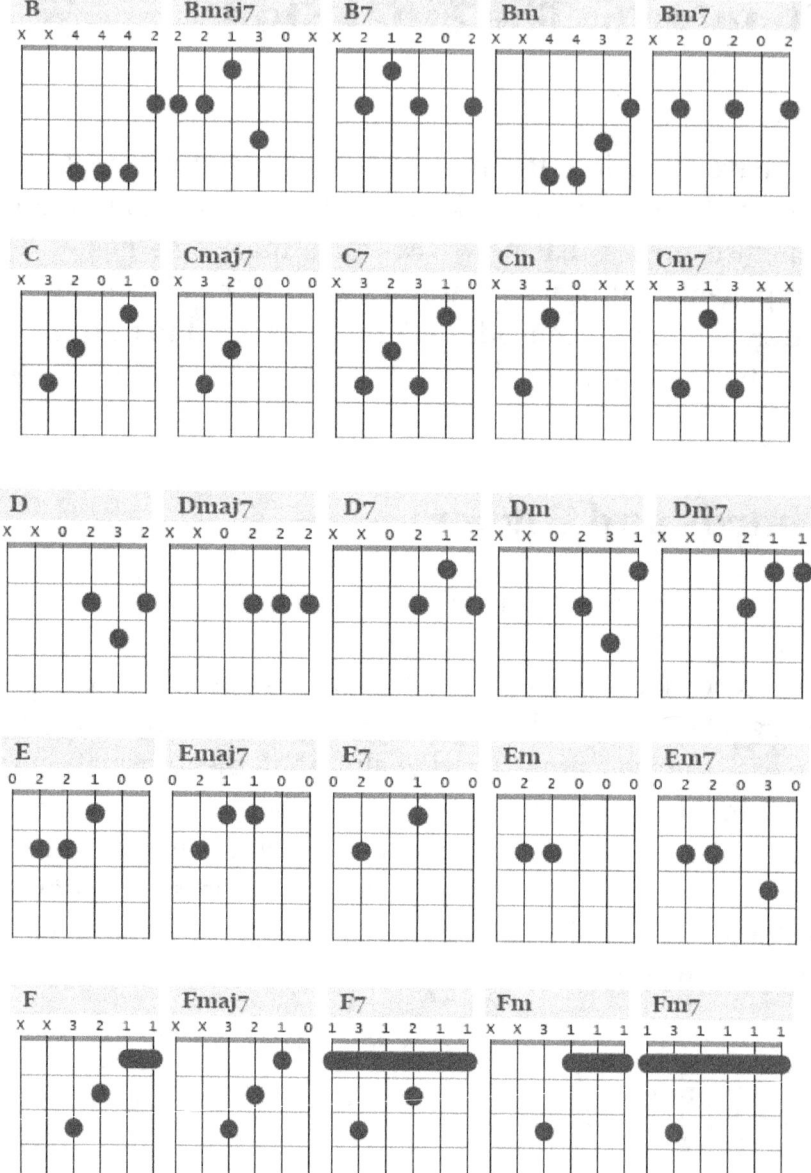

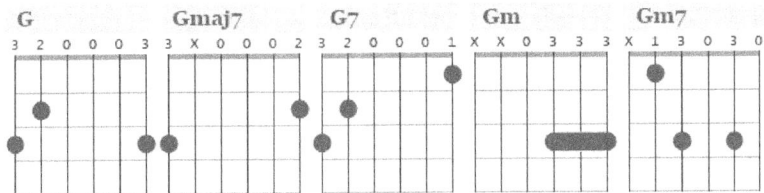

In most cases, you should have no problem playing these. However, the ones where you see a long bar can be tricky. The idea is to hold these fret positions using one finger. In most cases, that would be your index finger.

Apart from the ones above, you have the barre chords. All of these are played with the same principle of using the index finger to act as the new nut of the fretboard. As a result, this makes the shift of chords smaller.

The chord ensures that it follows its corresponding scale accordingly. An A major chord will follow the notes you find in the A major scale. For A minor, the appropriate changes will be made, so you would see a variation.

Important Chord Shapes

Before you go on to explore the barre chords, you need to know some important chord shapes. These shapes are simply carried forward, fret by fret, and the index finger shifts as the new nut, resulting in a barre chord.

There are E minor, E major, A major, and A minor, all in open positions. To reiterate, their respective positions are (from sixth to first/top to bottom):

E major

0 2 2 1 0 0

E minor

0 2 2 0 0 0

A major

0 0 2 2 2 0

A minor

0 0 2 2 1 0

Using these chords, you can move a fret up, and that would essentially change the chord by half a semitone. You can move anywhere on the fretboard using the same position.

For example, if you move the E minor chord position by a semitone (one fret), the chord changes to F minor, and so on. The same goes for chords played using other positions. This allows us to use all the notes and chords on the neck with great ease, further diversifying our songs and compositions.

Harmony

Harmony is when two or more notes are played together at the same time. Yes, a chord works the same way, but this is slightly different. Harmony involves using the chord, its construction, and the progression.

The entire concept of harmony is to lift the song or a piece to new heights. If done correctly, the harmony that is created is both unique and powerful.

Harmony uses the notes from the corresponding scale. Suppose if a song is using a C major key, harmony would use the notes within the said key and scale, but instead of playing C, you might play any other note within the same scale. When done simultaneously with another instrument, which may be playing the fifth note, and you the third, you end up with a completely new feel and sound. This form of harmony is called diatonic harmony. If you use notes which are not a part of the master scale, you will end up with a jazz feel to the song. This form of harmony is referred to as Non-diatonic harmony.

Atonal harmony is the third type of harmony. This form does not contain a tonal center, and nor is the root identifiable. It may sound a bit weird, but it was made popular in the free jazz movement, and many great artists used this technique to perform their songs. This involves using all 12 pitches as harmonies.

Practicing harmony is not easy, but once you start using them, you would find it hard to go back. Many bands and artists in existence today continue to use harmonies to further amplify the feel of the song, and to make the music more dominant.

Circle of fifths

This can seem a bit daunting at first, but once you understand how to use the circle of fifths, you will be composing songs with significant ease.

Every major key has a relative minor, and that is always true. Both use the same key signature as well (the number of sharps or flat signs, or lack thereof). Here is a look.

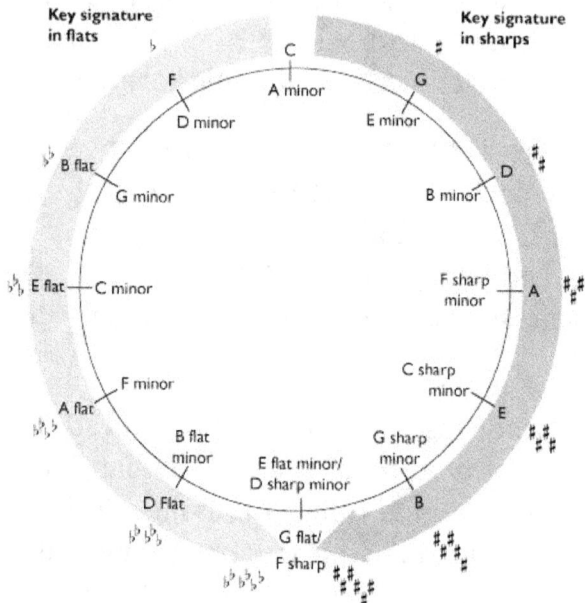

In the circle shown above, the keys on top of the ring are majors, and the ones underneath each are their relative minors. We know by practice that C major has no key signature (flat or sharp sign). The same is the case with its relative minor, which is A minor.

The circle of fifths is a sequence of different notes, separated by intervals of perfect fifths (Simplifying Theory, n.d.).

As you start to progress downwards, the number of key signatures begin to add up. If you go clockwise, you will start seeing more sharp signs, and if you go anti-clockwise, you will see more flat signs.

The circle of fifths is used to identify the key of the song. Simply count the number of key signatures, use this chart and move in the corresponding direction. You should always start from C. Start anywhere else, and you would end up getting the wrong results. You can also use this as a songwriter, to create more catchy melodies. Simply choose a key to work with, and identify the seven natural chords within that key. You can then start the progression using a chord of your choice and then build on the chord next to it, and their respective relative minors.

Circle of Fourths

This is effectively the circle of fifths written in reverse order.

```
                    C
             G      a      F
               e         d
         D       1♯    1♭      B♭
          b                  g
            2♯             2♭
       A  f♯ 3♯                 3♭ c  E♭
                 4♯        4♭
           E  c♯              f  A♭
                 5♯        5♭
                  g♯   6♯/6♭  b♭
                    B  d♯/e♭  D♭
                       F♯/G♭
```

There is no difference when it comes to the usage of these two circles. Both are opposites of each other. One primarily moves clockwise to indicate the number of sharps, and then eventually converted into flats, while the other does the opposite. You can rest assured that both would provide you with the same result. However, since these two exist, you must know them.

Songwriting with Modes

So far, you have learned almost everything you need to get started on your own songs. However, there is still one more thing which I would suggest you learn. These are called modes, and they can greatly help you in achieving exceptional results.

A mode is primarily a type of scale that has a distinct melodic characteristic. There are seven modes in existence:

1. Ionian
2. Dorian
3. Phrygian
4. Lydian
5. Mixolydian
6. Aeolian
7. Locrian

Before we learned how to divide an octave into 12 pitches, or notes, we, the musicians, had to rely on an imperfect system, and that is where these came to the rescue. Instead of having a single scale, there were seven modes used, each with their own structures.

Using modes allows us to obtain various feels and colors of music. The chart below uses the C major scale as the starting point. When played normally, or C to C, we end up getting the first mode (Ionian). However, when you change the starting key to D, you will end up at D, and this is where your intervals also start to change.

Mode	Quality	Example in C	Intervallic Pattern	Works over...
Ionian	Major		T T S T T T S	Major Triads Major Sevenths
Dorian	Minor		T S T T T S T	Minor Triads Minor Sevenths
Phrygian	Minor		S T T T S T T	Minor Triads Minor Sevenths
Lydian	Major		T T T S T T S	Major Triads Major Sevenths
Mixolydian	Major		T T S T T S T	Major Triads Dominant 7ths
Aeolian	Minor		T S T T S T T	Minor Triads Minor Sevenths
Locrian	Diminished		S T T S T T T	Diminished Triads m7b5 Chords

Notice how the intervals keep changing. By doing so, we create a different feel, and using the appropriate triads or chords we further amp up the feel of our songs with relative ease.

It takes practice and time. Practice as much as you can, and soon everything within this book will come to life and serve you for years to come. To help you along, here are 12 important tips to further your songwriting journey.

1. Start writing songs now - There is no point in waiting.
2. Sing your songs, even if you can't sing - We have all been there, but I assure you it will boost your confidence.
3. Learn how to play guitars and sing at the same time.
4. Go through your music theory.
5. Memorize the fretboard.
6. Train your ear to know what you are listening to.
7. Write as many original lyrics as you can - The more you write, the better you become.
8. Sing your own lyrics.
9. Songwriter's block will go away - Do not fear it.

10. Write as many songs as you can - You never know which ones may go on to break records.
11. Start songs from different places - Start with a riff, or with vocals, or all at once.
12. Write with other musicians - Always helps in providing a fresh new take on music.

Conclusion

The world of music theory cannot be described or summarized quickly and it continues to evolve every single day. Now and then, new techniques, rules, and regulations come into existence. So it would be difficult to compile all of that knowledge into something as short and concise.

My goal was to get you up to speed with the essentials. The purpose of the book was to ensure you know:

- How to read music
- About the numerous symbols and figures
- How to read tablatures
- Rhythms and arpeggios
- The variety of scales
- How to incorporate scales into playing

Not only do you now know more about guitar music, but you can confidently set out to pursue more advanced lessons, techniques, and exercises. As long as you keep practicing, the journey ahead will be nothing short of amazing.

Songwriting is fun, intuitive, and it requires the use of your creativity. Furthermore, playing your own music on guitar makes the journey that much more rewarding. By practicing and exploring the vast reaches of music you will find what fascinates you and catches your attention so you can write the song hiding inside your mind.

Throughout the book, I used images that may have served more as cheat sheets than anything, but that's okay. I want you to go out there and be able to pick up the pace. I do not want you to wait and try to learn for years before coming up with a song.

Why wait when you can do it now?

You have all you need to get going. Wherever you are, whatever your path may bring, I want to hear from you. If this book has taught you something useful, let me know through feedback. It is through positive feedback that I gain the courage to continue writing. I have so much more to share with you, but I can only do so if I know my books are helping my fellow musicians.

I wish you the best of luck, and I hope to hear your melodious work soon!

Discover "How to Find Your Sound"

http://musicprod.ontrapages.com/

Swindali music coaching/Skype lessons.

Email djswindali@gmail.com for info and pricing

References

Guitar Chalk Magazine. (2017, July 4). Guitar Scales Explained with Graphics and Clear Music Theory. *Medium*. https://medium.com/@guitar_chalk/guitar-scale-theory-1e5e39710137

Klaus Crow. (2014a, March 15). *The 5 Major Scale CAGED Shapes - Positions - GUITARHABITS*. GUITARHABITS. https://www.guitarhabits.com/the-5-major-scale-caged-shapes-positions/

Klaus Crow. (2014b, August 17). *The 5 Natural Minor Scale Positions You Must Know - GUITARHABITS*. GUITARHABITS. https://www.guitarhabits.com/the-5-natural-minor-scale-positions-you-must-know/

Simplifying Theory. (n.d.). *All about the Circle of Fifths and Fourths | Simplifying Theory*. Simplifying Theory. https://www.simplifyingtheory.com/circle-of-fifths-and-circle-of-fourths/

www.ingramcontent.com/pod-product-compliance
Lightning Source LLC
Chambersburg PA
CBHW071543080526
44588CB00011B/1777